James Cook

Shaun McCarthy

Heinemann
LIBRARY

H www.heinemann.co.uk/library
Visit our website to find out more information about **Heinemann Library** books.

To order:
- ☎ Phone 44 (0) 1865 888066
- 📄 Send a fax to 44 (0) 1865 314091
- 🖥 Visit the Heinemann Bookshop at www.heinemann.co.uk/library to browse our catalogue and order online.

First published in Great Britain by Heinemann Library,
Halley Court, Jordan Hill, Oxford OX2 8EJ,
a division of Reed Educational and Professional Publishing Ltd.
Heinemann is a registered trademark of Reed Educational and Professional Publishing Ltd.

OXFORD MELBOURNE AUCKLAND
JOHANNESBURG BLANTYRE GABORONE
IBADAN PORTSMOUTH (NH) USA CHICAGO

Designed by AMR
Illustrated by Art Construction
Originated by Ambassador Litho Ltd
Printed by Wing King Tong

ISBN 0 431 10489 1
06 05 04 03 02
10 9 8 7 6 5 4 3 2 1

British Library Cataloguing in Publication Data
McCarthy, Shaun
James Cook. – (Groundbreakers)
1.Cook, James, 1728–1779 2.Explorers – Great Britain –
Biography – Juvenile literature
I.Title
910.9'2

Acknowledgements
The publishers would like to thank the following for permission to reproduce photographs:
Armagh Observatory: p. 14; Art Archive: p. 34; Bridgeman Art Library: pp. 4, 20, 21, 28, 36, 39; Bridgeman/Coram Foundation: p. 11; Bridgeman/Department of Environment: p. 30; Bridgeman/Lincolnshire County Council; p. 24; Bridgeman/Mitchell Library: p.25; Bridgeman/National Gallery of Victoria: p. 22; Bridgeman/National Library of Australia: p. 5; Bridgeman/National Maritime Museum; p. 19; by kind permission of commanding Officer, HMS *Victory*: p. 10; Corbis: pp. 6, 21, 32, 41; Fotomas: p. 13; Hulton: pp. 33, 37; Mary Evans: p. 40; National Maritime Museum: pp. 9, 12, 15, 18, 26, 27, 29; National Portrait Gallery: p. 8; Stapleton Collection: pp. 16, 17, 31, 35; Whitby Museum: p. 7; Woodfall Wild Images: p. 23.

Cover photograph reproduced with permission of Corbis.

Every effort has been made to contact copyright holders of any material reproduced in this book. Any omissions will be rectified in subsequent printings if notice is given to the publishers.

Our thanks to Christopher Gibb for his comments in the preparation of this book.

Disclaimer
All the Internet addresses (URLs) given in this book were valid at the time of going to press. However, due to the dynamic nature of the Internet, some addresses may have changed, or sites may have ceased to exist since publication. While the author and publishers regret any inconvenience this may cause readers, no responsibility for any such changes can be accepted by either the author or the publishers.

Any words appearing in the text in bold, **like this**, are explained in the glossary.

Contents

Discovery and empire

Imagine a map of the world without Australia. The Pacific would then be a massive expanse of empty ocean. Many people thought this was how the world was when James Cook was born in 1728. His three voyages of discovery were to transform our knowledge of the world.

Sailing and navigating

Eighteenth-century sailing ships were at the mercy of the weather. Ships blown off course sometimes came upon undiscovered islands or were wrecked on unknown rocks. Cook was away for over three years on each of his voyages of discovery. He hardly spent any time at home with his family.

Cook was a brilliant sailor and navigator. He was interested in **astronomy** and in using the stars to find a course. He wrote many articles on how to navigate that were used by others.

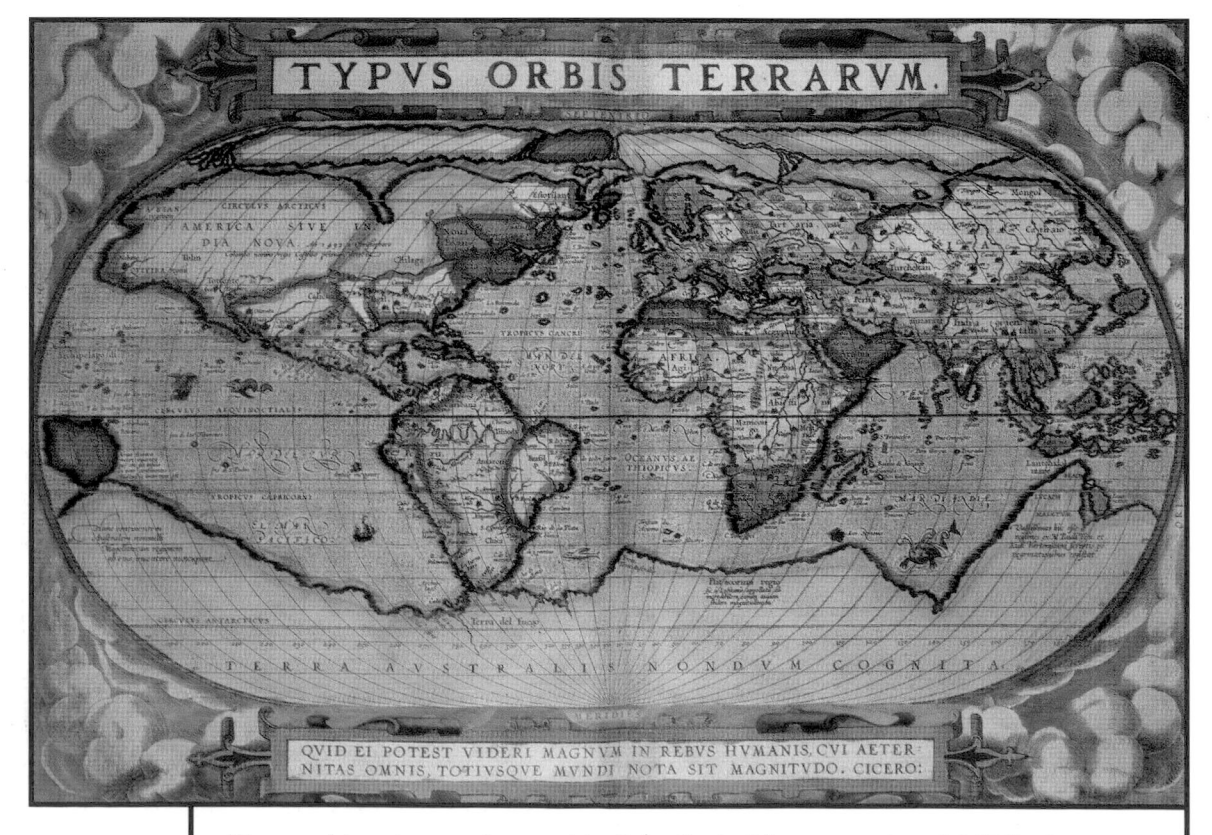

The world as it was mapped before Cook. This map, dated 1598, shows Australia as a massive continent in the southern hemisphere, and northern Canada is not quite right!

Mapping and claiming territory

The Navy was keen to find undiscovered islands and claim them for Britain so that ships (especially British ones!) could land there and pick up fresh supplies. They wanted the best **charts** to give their captains the advantage in any war.

Cook was one of the first Europeans to set foot on Australia. He was the first European to visit and map a huge number of Pacific islands. He made such accurate charts of the east coast of Canada that some of them were used by sailors even in the 20th century.

On all his voyages of discovery, his ships never fired a cannon in anger. But on the first voyage alone, Cook secured more territory for Britain than the whole Navy ever did in any single naval battle. Although Cook was a Navy captain, he was an explorer, not a fighter.

Captain Cook painted in 1776, the year in which he set off on his last voyage.

Science and discovery

All of Cook's voyages had scientists on board, usually astronomers and **naturalists**, and Cook took a keen interest in their work. Cook and the scientists did not just find new parts of the world, they recorded and interpreted what they found there.

An ordinary man of humble birth, Cook achieved greatness and fame through his skill, daring and humanity alone.

In the Commander's words:

'[He was] the ablest and most renowned navigator this or any other country hath produced. He possessed all the qualifications requiste for his profession and great undertakings.'

(From a letter written by Lord Pallister, Commander of the **Admiralty**, just after Cook's death in 1799)

The Cook family's cottage, which was shipped stone by stone to Melbourne, Australia, and rebuilt as a monument to the great sea captain.

James Cook was born on 27 October 1728 in the small Yorkshire village of Marton. His father was probably Scottish and worked as a farm labourer. His mother was Grace Pace, a Yorkshire woman. James was one of eight children, five of whom died. James was their only surviving son.

Soon after James was born the Cooks moved to a nearby village, Great Ayton. Here they farmed land owned by Thomas Skottowe, the local lord of the manor.

COOK'S FIRST SUPPORTER

Thomas Skottowe was Cook's first and most important **benefactor**. He was not an **aristocrat** and did not live in a great country house. However, his lifestyle at the manor would have been far grander than that of the poor people, such as James Cook's family, who worked his land and lived in cottages he owned.

Nevertheless, Skottowe was a kind and benevolent man. After Cook had gone to sea and left Yorkshire far behind, Skottowe helped to recommend him to the Navy as a gifted sea captain.

Boys of James Cook's humble social class did not receive much education in those days. Many never learned to write more than their own names or to do a few simple sums. Skottowe recognized that James was good at maths and arranged for him to attend the local school when he was seven years old.

Going to sea

Educated or not, James soon had to earn a living to help his family. When thirteen years old, he was **apprenticed**, with Skottowe's help, to the keeper of a general store in Staithes, a busy port on the Yorkshire coast. Staithes harbour was full of boats, and it must have been here that the young James Cook decided that life behind a shop counter was not for him.

Accounts of his going to sea are rather vague. Some say he ran away to sea, breaking the rules of his apprenticeship. Others say that the shop owner saw that his young apprentice was not cut out to spend his days serving customers. What is known is that when he was seventeen, he walked over the moors to Whitby, a larger port, and offered his services to the **mate** of a **collier** docked there. The mate sent him to the ship's owners, Walker Brothers of Whitby, who took him on. His long life at sea had begun.

A painting of Whitby harbour in the 1700s, where Cook first went to sea.

The Walkers' ships carried coal between Newcastle and London, sailing down the east coast of England. In the 18th century, all heavy goods were carried by sea, river or canal, as roads were bad and railways had not yet been invented.

Cook first went to sea on the **collier** *Freelove*. Although they were dirty, colliers were strong, seaworthy vessels, built to withstand storms. They were flat-bottomed so they could sail in and out of tidal harbours. Cook was to remember these qualities later on when planning his worldwide expeditions.

A portrait of James Cook. It did not take Cook many years to rise through the ranks, both on merchant ships and, later, in the Royal Navy.

Gaining experience

Cook helped in **rigging** a new Walker ship, the *Three Brothers*. In winter, when storms made sailing impossible, Cook helped clean and repair the Walker fleet. He spent long winter evenings with other **apprentice** sailors, learning the skills they would need to command their own vessels. Cook was a keen and gifted student of all things to do with sailing and the sea.

Cook gained his **mate**'s certificate. On **merchant ships** like the Walkers', the mate was responsible for seeing that orders issued by the captain were carried out. As mate, Cook had to understand everything about sailing a ship and commanding the crew. He did his new job well, and was soon due for promotion to **master** (captain of a merchant ship).

A Navy man

In 1755, James Cook decided to volunteer for the Royal Navy as an able seaman, almost the lowest rank of sailor. It was very unusual for anyone to turn down the chance to command his own merchant ship in order to start again at the bottom in the Navy. But Cook knew he could only be certain of acceptance in the Navy if he took a low rank.

In 1756 the Seven Years' War broke out. It would not be too long before Cook would see **active service** on a fighting ship.

Britain and France had claimed and **colonized** different parts of North America in the 17th and 18th centuries. They began fighting over territory there in 1754. The war was fought mainly across Canada, but then spread back into Europe in 1756, where it soon involved other countries. Two **alliances** formed: France, Austria, Russia, Sweden and Saxony against Britain, Prussia and Portugal. The Seven Years' War ended after Russia switched sides and joined Britain, Prussia and Portugal to defeat the French alliance.

Deptford naval dockyard, London, painted in the 18th century. Two Royal Navy 'men o' war,' fighting ships, are being made ready for sea.

The British people were proud of the Royal Navy, the most powerful naval force in the world in the mid-1700s. But it was very hard for commanders to find crews!

Officers and ordinary sailors

The Navy's 'ships of the line', their big fighting vessels, needed huge crews to sail them and man their rows of cannons. Pay was bad (unless there was **prize money** from captured ships), conditions on board were hard, and discipline was brutal. Sailors were **flogged** for breaking ship rules. 'Jumping ship' and running away was a **capital offence**.

Many ordinary sailors were press-ganged: kidnapped, often when asleep after getting drunk, from public houses around ports and made to sail in the Navy for years. They were kept almost like prisoners on board their ships by **marines**, soldiers who fought against crews of enemy ships in battle, but who also guarded the Navy ships and their crews when they were in harbour.

Officers usually came from influential or **aristocratic** families. To wear the uniform of a naval officer was a mark of status. These men often bought their **commissions**, whether or not they were actually any good at commanding ships!

The gun deck of a Royal Navy fighting ship. Six men worked each gun. Imagine the scene when all guns were firing.

An unusual recruit

When he volunteered for the Navy, Cook was already an experienced sailor. His enthusiasm and skills were noticed by commanding officers; he gained promotions and quickly rose through the ranks. In 1757, two years after joining the Navy, Cook was made **master** of HMS (His Majesty's Ship) *Pembroke*. In the Navy, a master was the officer in charge of navigation, not the captain, as on a **merchant ship**. Master was the highest **non-commissioned** post a seaman in the Navy could attain.

A good commander

Because Cook had started naval life as an able seaman, he was sympathetic towards the hardships sailors had to endure on board ship. Although he would punish sailors to maintain discipline on his ships, he was far less brutal than many naval captains. He was known to be fair to men under his command throughout his life. Many sailors signed up for voyage after voyage on ships under his command.

In 1759, he was made master of HMS *Northumberland*. In the same year, as master of HMS *Mercury*, Cook was sent across the Atlantic to join a naval fleet, commanded by Admiral Saunders, that was besieging the French-occupied Canadian city of Quebec.

Cook's first mission in Canada was to make **charts** of the St Lawrence River, right up to the French lines at Quebec. Because of the fighting, he had to work at night, but the charts he made were excellent. He was often in danger: once, armed Native Americans fighting for the French jumped into the **stern** of his boat as he jumped off the **bow**.

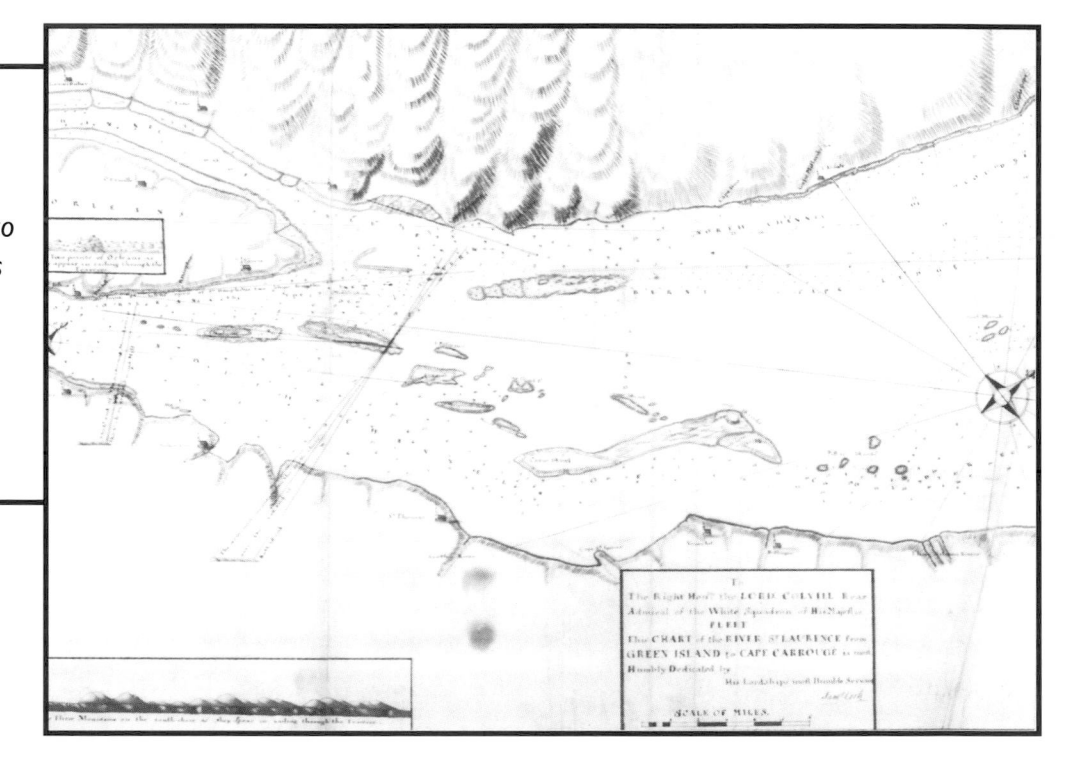

Part of Cook's charts of the St Lawrence. He often had to make his maps of the river at night.

The charts Cook made here and at other places along the Canadian coast were so accurate they were a major factor in the British finally winning the Seven Years' War. Indeed, the charts Cook made in Canada remained in use by some sailors into the 20th century.

THE BATTLE OF QUEBEC, 1759

Cook's charts of the St Lawrence River were vital in helping the British land their forces under the cliffs close to where the French were camped outside Quebec. The British scaled the cliffs and defeated the French on the Plains of Abraham above. The British commander, James Wolfe (1727–59), was killed in the battle but became a national hero. The battle was celebrated as a great victory in Britain.

An artist's impression of the Battle of Quebec, painted in the late 1700s.

Showing his talents

Cook was gaining a public reputation as a gifted surveyor and **cartographer**, and as a brave commander. This was unusual, as many civilians regarded Navy officers as rather simple, straightforward men of action. Cook was contributing scientific papers to the foremost group of thinkers in Britain at that time, the **Royal Society**. One of his better-known papers was on a complex method he had worked out for finding locations by observing the Moon.

Much of the world was not mapped in Cook's time, and navigation at sea was a hit-and-miss affair where errors could have fatal consequences. Many ships sank because they got lost and ran onto rocks. Devising better ways of navigating was a vital issue for the Navy, and Cook's ideas were discussed and admired at the highest level.

Marriage

In 1762, Cook met Elizabeth Batts while in England on leave. She was much younger than him, and from the lower professional class. They married just before Christmas, only weeks after meeting. Four months later, Cook sailed back to Canada leaving his wife in their house in East London. Elizabeth was to see very little of her husband in the years to come, only in the short periods between his voyages.

In 1767, the **Admiralty**, in association with the **Royal Society**, was planning an expedition to the South Pacific. Much of this expanse of ocean had not yet been explored by Europeans. They did not even know of the existence of Australia.

Watching the stars

The principal aim of the voyage was to take **astronomers** to observe a 'transit of Venus' from the Pacific island of Tahiti. However, in the 18th century an expedition into uncharted waters had to be prepared for anything.

THE TRANSIT OF VENUS

How far is the Sun from the Earth? One way to solve this is by observing the way the planet Venus moves across the face of the Sun, rather like the Moon does in a lunar eclipse. By recording the differences between the 'transit of Venus' viewed from two places on Earth as far apart as possible, astronomers can use a complex calculation to work out the distance to the Sun.

Today, astronomers can use computer models to calculate this without leaving their desks. But in the 18th century, the only way was to position observers in such remote places as Tahiti.

The Navy had the best ships and sailors for a long-distance expedition. They could also claim any discovered lands for the British crown. The Royal Society could provide the best scientists and astronomers to sample and record anything discovered along the way.

A page from Cook's notebook showing the phases of the transit of Venus, and a few drawings of animals. In an age before cameras, detailed drawings had to be made. Due to their age, much detail has been lost.

A strange choice?

The expedition attracted great public interest. It was usual for the captains of naval ships to be selected from men of the **aristocracy**. Many people were shocked that James Cook was chosen by the Navy to lead this voyage.

Cook, just 39 years old, was young to be a captain and unknown to the public, unlike the leaders of earlier naval expeditions. However, his interest in astronomy and skills as navigator and **cartographer** were recognized to be of vital importance for such a long and dangerous mission.

The *Endeavour*

On Cook's advice, the Admiralty bought a small Whitby **collier**, the *Earl of Pembroke*. He knew colliers were strong and manoeuvrable. On 3 April 1768, she was put into the Navy dockyard at Deptford on the Thames for refitting (improvement). Her hull was strengthened with extra planks, to protect her from tropical sea worms that ate into wooden ships. Her masts and **spars** were renewed. A month later, she had been made ready for the voyage and was re-named the *Endeavour*.

A model of the Endeavour, *in the National Maritime Museum, Greenwich, London. The refitted collier was nearly 30 metres long and weighed 393 tonnes.*

On 27 May 1768, Cook hoisted his captain's pennant above the *Endeavour* to show he was now in command. His ship would be home to 71 crew, 12 **marines**, 11 scientists and their servants for 3 years. On 30 July, they sailed down the Thames and headed west, anchoring off Plymouth on 13 August.

The 'great southern continent'

Cook did not tell his crew he had a second, secret, set of orders, which he was not to open until the voyage was under way. After the *Endeavour* left Plymouth on 26 August, Cook announced they were to go on from Tahiti to look for the 'great southern continent'.

Scientists at that time believed this existed in the South Pacific somewhere between the East Indies and the South Pole to counterbalance the weight of the continents in the Northern Hemisphere. Imagine how the crew must have felt as they learnt they were going on into the unknown to look for a new continent.

YOU CAN FOLLOW THE ROUTE OF COOK'S FIRST EXPEDITION ON THE MAP ON PAGES 42–3.

In Cook's words:

'While we lay waiting for a wind, the articles of war [the rules under which Navy crews sailed] and the act of Parliament were read to the ship's company, who were paid two months wages in advance, and told that they were to expect no additional pay for the performance of the voyage.'

(A passage from Cook's log, implying they should not expect **prize money**)

Sydney Parkinson was an artist on the voyage. This sketch shows his record of animals he had seen.

The *Endeavour* sailed across the Atlantic, arriving in Rio de Janeiro, Brazil, on 13 November and then south to Cape Horn. The 'Horn', feared by all sailors as a place of storms and huge waves, was calm when they slipped round into the Pacific.

30 AUGUST – '*A storm in the Atlantic. Many chickens [kept for fresh eggs] lost overboard ...*'

25 OCTOBER – '*Crossing the Equator. All those who have not crossed it before must be dunked over the side, tied to a chair [a sailing custom]. Banks [the expedition's **naturalist**] pays a ransom of four days' wine allowance to get himself, his servants, dogs and cat let off.*'

17 JANUARY, ashore at Tierra del Fuego – '*Banks and others go on a collecting expedition. It is freezing cold. They lose their way ... spend a night out in the open, but make it back to the ship.*'

A pen and ink sketch of the Endeavour *in rough seas, by Sydney Parkinson.*

YOU CAN FOLLOW THE ROUTE OF COOK'S FIRST EXPEDITION ON THE MAP ON PAGES 42–3.

As the *Endeavour* sailed through the South Pacific, the temperature and humidity increased, making life on the crowded ship even more uncomfortable. Books and paper grew mouldy and iron started to rust. Finally, on 13 April 1769, they dropped anchor in Port Royal, Matavia Bay, Tahiti. Several European ships had landed briefly at Tahiti before 1769, but Cook's expedition was the first to spend any length of time there and to map and describe the island.

A view of Tahiti by one of the expedition's artists Sydney Parkinson, with the Endeavour *safely anchored in a bay. Cook was to visit the island many times, and make many friends there.*

New supplies

The crew watched anxiously as local people rowed canoes out to the ship. Cook recognized that the local people were friendly, and wanted to trade. He took on breadfruit, coconuts, bananas and fish in exchange for coloured beads and manufactured goods. He was keen for his men to have as much fresh food as possible as he knew it would prevent them from contracting **scurvy**.

Through May and June the crew relaxed. Relations between them and the islanders were good, and very good between some of the crew and the women of Tahiti. Two of the twelve **marines** tried to desert when the ship was getting ready to leave in July, because they wanted to stay with women they had met. They were both captured and forced to continue the voyage. Relationships with island women were not limited to the ordinary sailors. Joseph Banks of the **Royal Society** fought a pistol duel with the ship's surgeon over a woman: they both missed!

Scurvy is a disease of the blood caused mainly by a lack of vitamin C, usually found in fresh fruit and vegetables. The first signs are usually bleeding gums, followed by a quick decline into lethargy, and then often death. It was a major killer on ships in the days before refrigeration and canning, when sailors on long voyages existed on a poor diet of mostly stale, salted and dried food. In the whole of the Seven Years' War (1756–63), it is estimated that only 1512 sailors were killed in battles, but 133,708 died from diseases, mainly scurvy.

Success

On 3 June, the transit of Venus was successfully observed. The telescope was mounted, the exact time of the transit carefully noted using an astrological clock, and everything was painstakingly written down. Having completed the first part of their mission, they were now to sail on into the unknown.

These are Tahitian war canoes, painted by one of the expedition's official artists, William Hodges, but the islanders who rowed out to meet Cook's ship were friendly.

The 'great southern continent'

YOU CAN FOLLOW THE ROUTE OF COOK'S FIRST EXPEDITION ON THE MAP ON PAGES 42–3.

Cook left Tahiti on 13 July. The *Endeavour* had been away from home for nearly a year and the isolation was taking its toll on the crew. The ship's **log** records that on 28 August the boatswain's **mate** died 'after drinking three pints of neat rum'.

They sighted New Zealand on 6 October 1769. New Zealand had been discovered by the Dutch explorer Abel Tasman in 1642, but there were no complete maps of it. No one knew whether it was part of the 'great southern continent'.

A dangerous encounter

They sailed into Poverty Bay the next day. The coast looked so much like southern England that many of the crew felt homesick. However, the local people were not so familiar! **Maori** watched from the beach, then ran into the woods when Cook landed with a party of sailors.

This drawing of Maori war canoes is from the journal of Abel Tasman's voyage in search of the great southern continent.

ABEL TASMAN

Abel Janszoon Tasman (1603–c.59) was a Dutch sailor and explorer. Like Cook, he was sent in quest of the 'great southern continent'. In 1642, he discovered the area he named Van Diemen's Land (now Tasmania) and New Zealand, followed by Tonga and Fiji (1643). In 1644, he landed on the north-west coast of Australia. However, although he set foot on Australia over 130 years before Cook, he did not realize this was a vast landmass, nor did he claim it for the Dutch.

This painting by a member of Cook's crew shows an officer from the Endeavour trading with a Maori: a handkerchief for a crayfish!

Cook himself went into the woods looking for the Maori, hoping to trade. While his search party was gone, the Maori burst out of the trees, apparently ready to attack the sailors guarding the boats. They were armed with spears and clubs. Their shouting and tattooed faces terrified the sailors. After firing warning shots into the air, a sailor shot and killed one of the Maori. They halted their charge, picked up their dead comrade, and disappeared. Cook returned and the landing party returned to the ship.

Cannibals!

Cook tried again and again to make contact, but the Maori were now in a warlike mood. The crew became less inclined to leave the safety of the *Endeavour* when they discovered that some Maori were cannibal, who sometimes ate human flesh. However, trading of goods for fresh food was eventually done. On 15 November, Cook claimed New Zealand for Britain. Cook sailed along the coast of both islands that make up New Zealand, making accurate maps. He eventually realized this could not be the great, undiscovered continent. On 31 March 1770, Cook set sail for Van Diemen's Land (Tasmania), and home.

A gale drove the *Endeavour* south-east. On 19 April 1770, the crew sighted uncharted land and Cook looked for a place to anchor. On 28 April they set foot on Australia. Cook let his nephew, Isaac Smith, a 16-year-old **midshipman** on the *Endeavour*, be the first ashore. They claimed the whole of eastern Australia as British territory.

A 19th-century painting of Cook and his crew setting foot on Australia, 28 April 1770.

The shore was rich in fruit, vegetables and animals, so they named their landing site Botany Bay. They replenished their stores of food and water, and saw their first kangaroo. **Aborigines** were also seen on the shore, but they ran away from Cook's men. Sailing on up the coast, Cook found a large and beautiful bay. The city of Sydney stands here today, built around its world-famous natural harbour.

Shipwreck

They continued up the coast, surveying as they went. They did not know they were becoming trapped between the coast and the Great Barrier **Reef**. On 12 June, they ran aground on the reef. Cook ordered all unnecessary items to be thrown overboard to lighten the *Endeavour* and float her off the reef.

YOU CAN FOLLOW THE ROUTE OF COOK'S FIRST EXPEDITION ON THE MAP ON PAGES 42–3.

They soon realized the ship was badly holed and taking on water. As sailors pumped out the water, Cook desperately looked for somewhere to beach the *Endeavour* for repairs.

Sydney Harbour, which the crew of the Endeavour *first saw in 1770. The city that grew up around it now has a skyline recognized around the world.*

Repairs

After four days, Cook found a suitable place at a river mouth, which they named Endeavour River. With the ship out of the water, they set about repairing it with the simple tools they had. They cut timber from the shore and forged nails and bolts. Holes were plugged with sailcloth smeared with animal dung! On 4 August 1770, they set off again for home, this time aware of the dangers of the reef.

Homeward bound

On the long haul half-way round the world back to England, **scurvy** and **dysentery** began to attack the crew. The ship's **log** notes that eleven sailors died between 30 January and 6 February 1771 alone. Cook had tried to ensure his men's health, and these deaths must have distressed him. Finally, on 13 April 1771, the *Endeavour* sailed into Deal harbour in Kent.

The Cooks at home

We know a lot about Cook's voyages, but very little is known of Cook's home life. Once the *Endeavour* was safely docked in the Thames, Cook went to his house in Mile End in East London. He was reunited with Elizabeth and his two sons, who were called Nathaniel and James. Sadly, however, their daughter Elizabeth had died just three months before his return.

Cook was still only a **lieutenant** when he returned to England, but he was duly promoted permanently to the rank of captain. He did not receive as much public attention as the scientists such as Banks, who brought back exciting evidence of distant places and peoples.

Paperwork

Captains had to run their ships like businesses. After a voyage, there were forms to fill in describing the condition of the ship (Cook wrote simply 'foul'), letters of condolence to write to the families of men who had died, and wages to be paid to the crew. Cook sorted through the huge collection of curiosities he had gathered on the voyage, such as canoe paddles and native weapons. He gave many to his family. His pay for the entire voyage had been just 100 **guineas** (about £35 for each year he had spent at sea, although that would have bought a lot more than it does today).

In Cook's words:

'I flatter myself that [my reports] will convey a Tolerable knowledge of the places they are intended to illustrate and that the discoveries we have made, though not great, will Apologise for the length of the voyage.'

(Although writing in the formal style of the 18th century, Cook still sounds rather humble in this letter to his commanders at the Admiralty)

A painting of the scientist Sir Joseph Banks, with his tools and log book and items collected from his travels with Cook.

Another voyage?

The **Admiralty** realized the importance of Cook's discoveries. Cook knew he had found a great land mass, but did not know if this was the 'great southern continent'. Did that still lie undiscovered out there somewhere, further south towards the frozen wastes of Antarctica?

In the autumn of 1771, after only a few months at home, Cook received the order to 'complete the discovery of the Southern Hemisphere'. He would command a second expedition of two ships.

RESOLUTION AND ADVENTURE

Cook's new ships, the *Resolution* and the *Adventure*, were also converted **colliers**. An extra deck was added to the *Resolution* and a 'roundhouse' built on this. Joseph Banks was again to be the voyage's **naturalist** and he reserved the roundhouse to live and work on.

But sailing down the Thames things went wrong: the *Resolution* was top-heavy. At Sheerness, near the mouth of the river, **midshipman** John Elliot described in his diary:

'Two hundred shipwrights were cutting and tearing the ship to pieces ... In a few days they took away the Round House and made other alterations so as to render her lighter upwards.'

Banks was so upset at this, he refused to go on the voyage!

This watercolour of the Resolution *lying in calm water was painted by one of the crew, midshipman Henry Roberts. It captures the romance that many people felt surrounded Cook's voyages to the South Sea islands.*

Cook finally left England on 13 July 1772. He had stores to last two years, including a supply of lemons that he hoped would prevent **scurvy**. Sixteen of the *Resolution's* crew, loyal to Cook, were volunteers from his last voyage.

Harrison's revolutionary sea clock kept an accurate record of time whatever the sea conditions.

Cook had John Harrison's experimental sea clock on board. If Cook could keep an accurate record of the time elapsed since leaving port, he could fix his **longitude** accurately, and this would make navigation much more precise. The clock worked very well and helped Cook navigate vast distances out of sight of land.

Ice!

They sailed south, reaching the Cape of Good Hope on 29 October. This first leg of the voyage had taken 109 days. They had endured very bad weather and had almost run out of fresh water. Now, rounding the southern tip of Africa, they sailed due south into the Antarctic Circle. They had to keep constant watch for **icebergs**. Steering a sailing ship round these was not easy, but the crew was grateful for the fresh drinking water made available by melting ice from the icebergs.

You can follow the route of Cook's second expedition on the map on pages 42–3.

By December, they found themselves confronted by endless **pack ice**. They sailed along the edge for two months, looking for a break to sail further south, but found none. On 17 January 1773, they became the first ships to record crossing **latitude** 70 degrees south within the Antarctic Circle.

Lost in the fog

In February, Cook reported that they were sailing between 'islands of ice from half a mile to three miles long'. According to **midshipman** John Elliot, ice covered the **rigging** 'like compleat christal ropes'.

This painting by William Hodges captures all the drama of sailing in unknown waters between huge icebergs.

Cook ordered the *Adventure* to keep seven kilometres of clear water between herself and the *Resolution* to make manoeuvring around ice easier. But the two ships lost contact in fog. After firing a cannon at regular intervals but hearing no shot in reply, Cook suddenly found his way blocked by a wall of ice. He turned north and headed for the warmer climate of New Zealand, where the ships had arranged to meet if they became separated.

Chased by the Spanish:

'In sailing past Cape Finistère [off the French coast] we were Chased by two Spanish Men of War. The nearest, a Sixty four [64 guns], fired several shots at the Adventure, *to bring her to [make her stop], and Capt. Foneraux did bring to, which displeased Captain Cook, as he considered it an Insult to the British Flag. The Spaniard asked what ship that was ahead, and being told it was the* Resolution, *Capt. Cook, he said: "Oh, Cook is it?" and wished us all good voyage.'*

(From the diary of midshipman John Elliot)

Cook notes in his **log** that he 'was not backward in carrying sail [using a lot of sail] as well by night as by day', and the *Resolution* arrived in New Zealand on 26 March 1773. They had been on the frozen ocean for 117 days without sight of land. The *Adventure* eventually arrived too.

The local ruler, 'King Oree', welcomed them. The climate of New Zealand is similar to England's, and animals and plants they introduced all thrived. During the winter, Cook cruised through the islands of the South Pacific, discovering and naming many and claiming them for Britain.

YOU CAN FOLLOW THE ROUTE OF COOK'S SECOND EXPEDITION ON THE MAP ON PAGES 42–3.

Furthest south

In November 1773, Cook sailed south towards the ice once again. He reached the **pack ice** in December, again searched for a way through, but found none. On 30 January 1774, he reached the furthest south he could go, just 121 kilometres from the coast of Antarctica.

In Cook's words:

'Ice extended east and west far beyond the reach of our sight, while the southern half of the horizon was illuminated by rays of light which reflected from the ice to a considerable height.'

(This extract from Cook's journal hints at how awesome the scene must have been to the men in their tiny wooden ships)

Crewmen from the Resolution *hacked at floating ice to collect fresh drinking water.*

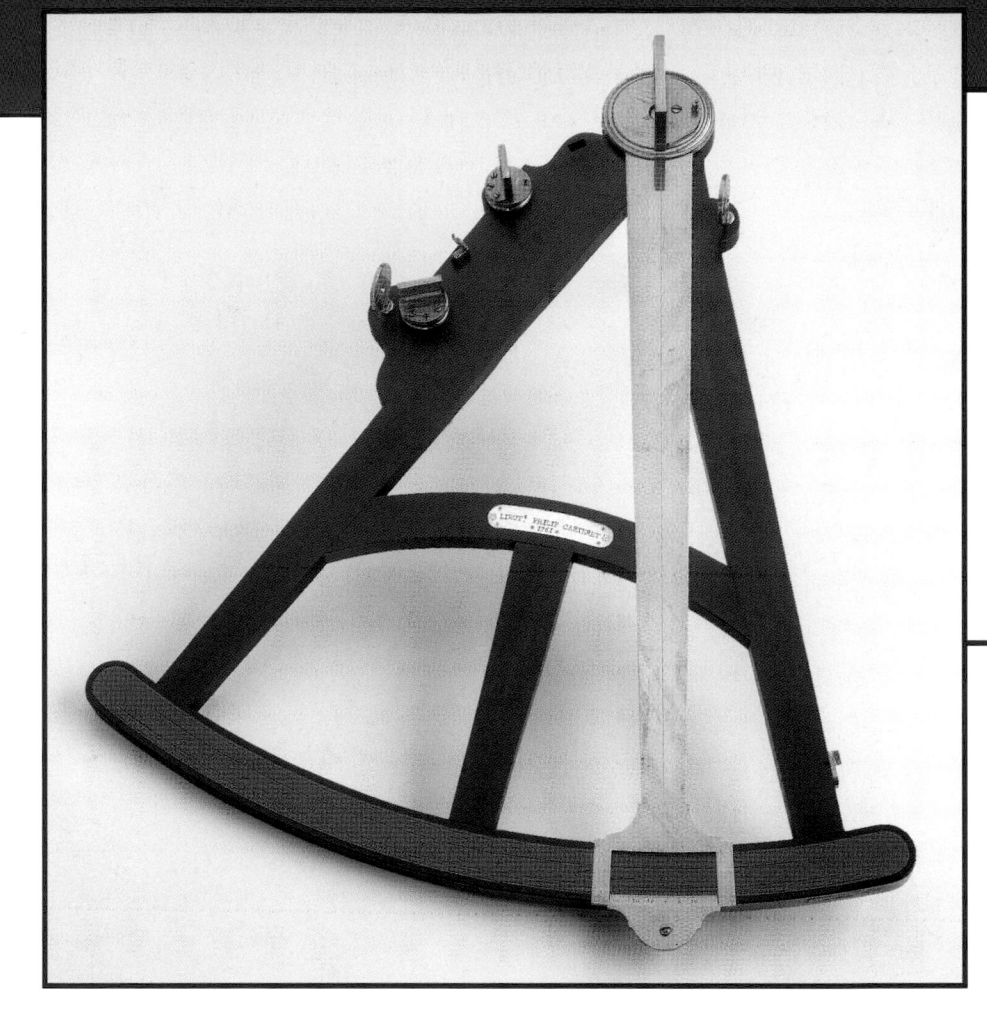

*Cook managed to navigate huge distances out of sight of land using simple instruments like this quadrant, which is used to gauge **latitude** by measuring the angle between the Sun and the horizon.*

Cook sailed south from New Zealand, across the southern ocean and across the Antarctic Circle. He proved there was no 'great southern continent', and that Australia was not connected to the South Pole. With winter beginning to freeze the seas around the ships, Cook headed back north to New Zealand, visiting the New Hebrides and the Cook Islands (named after him) on the way.

'CLAIMING' NEW TERRITORIES

European explorers saw newly (to them) discovered parts of the world as a series of prizes, to be 'claimed' for their home country. French, Spanish, Dutch and especially British navigators eagerly claimed territory all over the globe.

It is strange to consider that men like Cook, thousands of kilometres from home and with small crews, thought they could 'claim' land as vast as Australia and make it a 'possession' of Britain. A proclamation claiming the land was read out, the land was given a name and a flag was raised. No one bothered to ask the local 'natives' what they thought about it! Then the explorers would sail away and the newly claimed possession might not see another European – from the country that now supposedly owned it – for years.

Cook returned once again to Tahiti. After two voyages into the Antarctic, the islands of the South Pacific must have seemed like paradise to Cook's crews. What is more, the care with which Cook organized rations to prevent disease meant only one sailor died from illness during the whole voyage.

Homeward bound

YOU CAN FOLLOW THE ROUTE OF COOK'S SECOND EXPEDITION ON THE MAP ON PAGES 42–3.

Cook began the journey home in November 1774. It took five weeks to cross the South Pacific to Tierra del Fuego. Sailing east into the Atlantic, they came across an undiscovered, ice-covered island, which Cook named South Georgia. This must have rekindled Cook's love of exploration, for he changed course for the Antarctic once more. In January 1775, he found a desolate group of islands, which he named the South Sandwich Islands (after John Montague, Lord Sandwich, First Lord of the **Admiralty**).

An engraving by Sydney Parkinson, showing Cook's crew hunting sea lions for fresh meat. The animals were so unused to humans they did not try to escape.

They finally reached England on 30 July 1775. They had been away for three years and eighteen days. They had sailed more than 96,000 kilometres (60,000 miles), many of those through previously unexplored seas.

Recognition

This time the public recognized Cook's achievements. His reputation as a great navigator was assured. He had claimed further territory for Britain. In keeping disease at bay on such a long voyage, he had demonstrated what an intelligent and humane commander he was. He was especially popular with one set of businessmen: whalers. Cook's **log** constantly mentioned the great numbers of whales and seals he had seen. Whale ships hunted in the Arctic: now they would be tempted to go far south to the Antarctic to reap the rich harvest Cook had reported.

A drawing by Sydney Parkinson, who described this man as 'an Heiva, or Kind of Priest'.

WHALING

Hunting whales was big business in the 18th century. Whale oil was used in lamps that, along with candles, were the main form of lighting. Whalebone was used for a variety of purposes, including 'stays' in the corsets (tight, waist-gripping undergarments) women regarded as high fashion. Whaling was a dangerous business, with ships often at sea for years at a time. Sometimes a vessel would come back without a single catch, so Cook's description of the many whales he saw was a great temptation to whalers.

Cook now turned his attention to another great maritime quest: the North-west Passage. For several centuries, European ships had sailed to the East to profit from the spices, silk and other cargoes they found there. The only route was a long and dangerous voyage round Africa via the Cape of Good Hope. Navigators had tried to find a way in the 'other direction', sailing west from Europe 'over the top' of North America. This would involve a journey through the frozen Arctic seas. Over 50 attempts had been made to find a 'North-west Passage' from the Atlantic into the Pacific, but none had succeeded.

Cook had been promoted to a sort of semi-retirement ashore, but at 46 years old, he felt himself too young to give up his seafaring life. When the **Admiralty** began planning a voyage to search for the North-west Passage, they held a meeting of the most distinguished naval captains to discuss who would lead it.

In Cook's words:

'SIR, Having understood that their Lordships have ordered two ships to be fitted out for the purpose of making further discoveries in the Pacific Ocean, I take the liberty ... To submit myself to their directions, if they think fit to appoint me to the command on the said intended voyage ...'.

(From Cook's letter to the Admiralty, modestly confirming his interest in commanding a third voyage)

This portrait of Captain Cook is in the book he wrote about his voyage to Antarctica. As soon as he returned from that trip, he began planning his next expedition.

Cook was invited to attend and sat in the meeting listening. He then jumped up and offered his services as commander. Surprised, everyone agreed immediately.

Cook may have had another reason for offering to lead the voyage. The Government believed that the North-west Passage would give British ships such a trading advantage that they were offering £20,000 to whoever discovered it.

Henry Hudson, who died trying to find the North-west Passage.

Christmas on Kerguelen Island

YOU CAN FOLLOW THE ROUTE OF COOK'S THIRD VOYAGE ON THE MAP ON PAGES 42–3.

Cook's old ship the *Resolution* was refitted for the voyage. The *Adventure* was now **unseaworthy** and Cook was asked to find another ship. Again, he chose a **collier** and re-named it the *Discovery*. The ships left Plymouth on 12 July 1776. Cook had been at home in London with his wife and children for just under a year.

Cook's orders were to sail first to the Pacific islands he knew so well and then go north, to search for the North-west Passage from the Pacific to the Atlantic. This way of looking for the route had not been tried before by the Navy. The ships carried English farm animals and garden seeds for the South Sea islanders, as well as implements and gifts to trade.

The *Resolution* arrived at Cape Town on 18 October. She had not been well refitted and was leaking. The *Discovery* was blown off-course in a gale and did not arrive until 10 November. Cook, always aware of the dangers of disease caused by bad rations, ordered that every crewman should have fresh meat and vegetables every day. The sheep and cattle were landed to graze, but some were eaten by wild dogs, and others escaped.

Cook was keen to return to the islands he knew and loved in the South Pacific. This painting shows Tahitians dancing. Cook and his crew enjoyed being guests at celebrations like this.

Cook had difficulty rounding up the lost animals. Suspecting some might have been stolen, he hired 'some of the meanest and lowest scoundrels in the place' to look for them. Along with the ship's animals, he also took on board 'two young bulls, two heifers, two young horses, two mares, two rams, several ewes and goats, and some rabbits and poultry.' The ships must have resembled crowded Noah's arks.

Kerguelen Island

Cook had been ordered to explore Kerguelen, a barren and remote island south-east of Cape Town, which had been discovered four years previously by the French. They left Cape Town on 30 November and arrived at Kerguelen on 24 December.

Always a skilled **cartographer**, Cook fixed their exact position and set about mapping the island. He climbed a hill to survey the land but was repeatedly cut off by sudden dense fogs. The crew found what little grass there was on the island to cut to feed the animals. They killed seals for making oil for their lamps and birds for fresh meat. Cook noted that the men had 'wrought [worked] hard'. It was Christmas Day, 1776.

Cook's ships anchored below the inhospitable cliffs of remote Kerguelen Island.

Cook sailed on and made his usual stops at New Zealand and Tahiti. Animals that had survived the rough seas and freezing weather on the journey were unloaded.

Health matters

Cook tried many ways to encourage his crew to eat fresh food to stay healthy. He carried 'portable soup' (vegetable soup boiled down to a thick paste which could be kept for long periods) and spruce beer (a German beer made with pine tree needles). Many sailors were suspicious of strange foods. They refused to try sauerkraut (pickled cabbage, a German dish) until Cook served it to the officers. He also made the men wash as often as water supplies allowed, and air their hammocks every day.

Cook and the islanders

Cook was becoming a regular visitor to the Pacific islands and was popular with locals. He traded items from Europe for their abundant fresh food, and was known to give 'lifts' to people between islands. Some officers' journals even reported that local women lived on board ship. However much Cook enjoyed island life, though, he had a mission to complete.

A group of islands in the Pacific Ocean was named after Cook. This aerial photograph shows some of them, including the mountainous island of Rarotonga.

No way through

Cook sailed on towards the Pacific coast of North America, passing some of the smaller Hawaiian islands on the way. He then sailed up the west coast of Canada, round the tip of Alaska, through the Bering Strait and into the Arctic Ocean. He began looking for the North-west Passage, but every route he tried was blocked with ice.

With the Arctic winter setting in, Cook headed south to find a suitable place to repair his ships ready for another attempt at 'the passage' the following spring. He eventually found the island of Hawaii (which he called O'why'he).

YOU CAN FOLLOW THE ROUTE OF COOK'S THIRD VOYAGE ON THE MAP ON PAGES 42–3.

WILLIAM BLIGH

Cook, the most humane Navy captain of his day, had an officer aboard who was to become notorious as one of the most brutal. While serving under Cook, 21-year-old William Bligh was a trusted and capable officer. But years later, when he was captain of his own ship, the *Bounty*, Bligh was so cruel to his crew that they **mutinied**, took over the ship and cast him and several other officers adrift in an open boat in the middle of the Pacific. Bligh survived and the mutineers lived on an uncharted Pacific island for the rest of their lives. The mutiny on the *Bounty* remains the most famous in British naval history.

A portrait of William Bligh, who served as a young officer on Cook's expedition.

You can follow the route of Cook's third voyage on the map on pages 42–3.

Cook searched the Kona coast of Hawaii for a harbour in November and December 1779. He finally landed at Kealakekua Bay. The Hawaiians celebrated the seasons of different gods at different times of the year, and Cook's arrival coincided with the start of the season of a god called Lonoikamakahiki, or Lono makua. The islanders would make a procession in a clockwise direction round the island bearing banners of white cloth hung from a cross branch on a long pole. These were very like the square-rigged sails of Cook's ships, and the ships were moving along the coast in a clockwise direction.

A living god?

Did the Hawaiians think Cook was their god? He was welcomed ashore by High Chief Kaeo. Cook was led round their sacred sites. People fell on their faces at his feet. Cook was amazed, but he was used to encountering strange welcomes and ceremonies.

The last journey

Cook's final voyage was tragically short. He left Hawaii on 4 February 1779, but one of the *Resolution's* masts was damaged after only a week at sea. They returned to Kealakekua Bay. The timing was significant, for this was the end of the season of Lono makua, when the islanders symbolically sacrificed an image of the god.

This time, Cook received a very different welcome. The islanders were not openly hostile, but thefts and minor trouble became common. Items were stolen from the expedition. A **longboat** was taken and one of the sailors who had been guarding it was killed. On 14 February, Cook decided to hold the Hawaiian High Chief hostage on the *Resolution* until the longboat was returned (not knowing it had been burnt by the islanders, who wanted just its iron fittings).

A fatal misunderstanding

Cook had tried this hostage tactic on other islands where he was well known and liked. Usually the hostages came along quite willingly and the problem was easily resolved. Crucially, however,

Cook did not realize how serious things had become on Hawaii. The Chief at first agreed to be hostage and was led to the beach to be taken away. But his wife begged him not to get into Cook's **pinnace** (small boat) and scuffling broke out.

Cook's men opened fire, Cook was threatened with a knife and he fired his double-barrelled pistol, killing a Hawaiian. Serious fighting then broke out. Cook was clubbed down as he tried to clamber into the pinnace. Most of the sailors got off the beach but Cook and four **marines** lay dead on the sand.

Utterly demoralized by the death of their commander, the ships turned for home, arriving in England in August 1780.

This painting of Cook, made a few years after his death, is designed to make him appear heroic, showing him fighting single-handedly to protect his men against many attackers.

The Legacy of Captain Cook

Cook's three voyages set the British Royal Navy at the forefront of maritime exploration in the mid-1700s. His name is most often linked with the 'discovery' of the east coast of Australia, even though other men had landed, usually briefly, on Australian shores before him. His name is linked to the discovery of Australia because his visit was well recorded, he made accurate **charts** of the coast, and because Australia became a British possession.

The South Seas

Cook discovered and charted many South Pacific islands, including the Sandwich Islands, Tonga, the Cook Islands, and many islands in the Hawaiian group. His treatment of islanders was always humane – at least, by the standards of the time! He wrote in his journal that he had learned to 'manage the natives without taking away their lives'. In an age when explorers often attacked the natives of places they discovered, Cook's understanding of, and affection for, Pacific islanders was remarkable.

The Resolution *and the* Adventure *at Matavai Bay, Tahiti, where Cook so often returned. This painting by William Hodges, artist on the second voyage, captures the beauty and romance that Cook's voyages to the South Pacific conjured up for Europeans in the 18th century.*

(Sadly, the European diseases that sailors brought to the islanders proved fatal to many locals. Ailments that were not deadly to Europeans could kill an islander who had no immunity to the germs.)

A professional sailor

Cook often comes across in his writings as a man too **deferential** to his superiors. As a father and husband he was largely absent. However, as a naval captain he was supremely confident of his own abilities. He knew that no other man in the world at that time had his first-hand experience.

James Cook sailed his ships on three enormous voyages of discovery that many people thought impossible. His skills as a navigator and leader allowed those voyages to further our understanding of the world.

THE DISCOVERY OF AUSTRALIA

It is not known which European first 'discovered' Australia. It is said that a Spanish ship passed the Torres Strait in 1545. A Dutch ship sighted another part of the coast of the mysterious country in 1627. Vague records suggest that William Dampier was the first English explorer to set eyes on Australia, in 1688.

It is sad to think that what the humane Cook discovered was used for many years as a brutal prison colony where many **transported** prisoners died from barbaric ill-treatment.

The statue of James Cook at Anchorage, Alaska, USA, a point he passed on his search for the North-west Passage.

Map of Cook's voyages

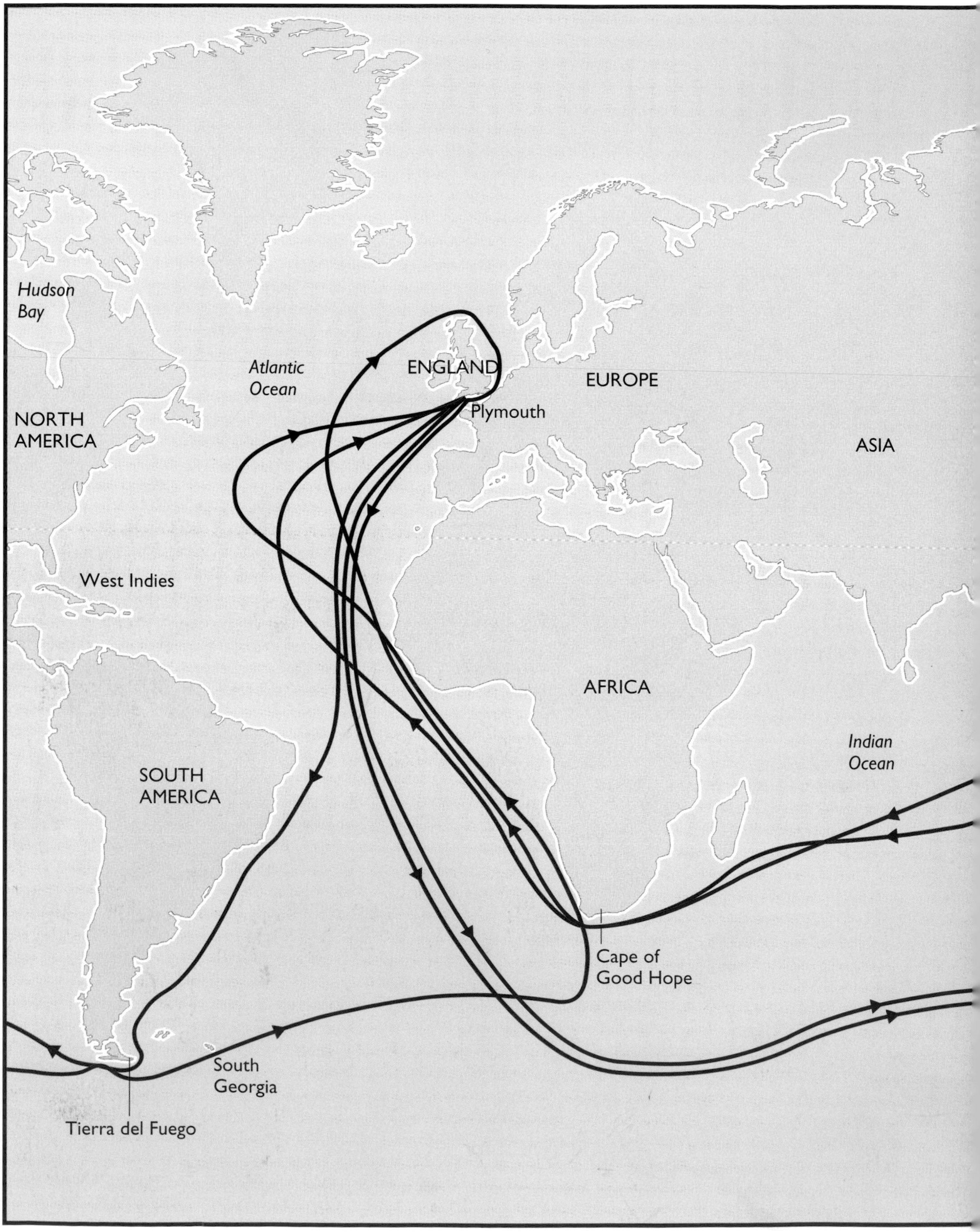

Hudson Bay
NORTH AMERICA
Atlantic Ocean
ENGLAND
Plymouth
EUROPE
ASIA
West Indies
AFRICA
Indian Ocean
SOUTH AMERICA
Cape of Good Hope
South Georgia
Tierra del Fuego

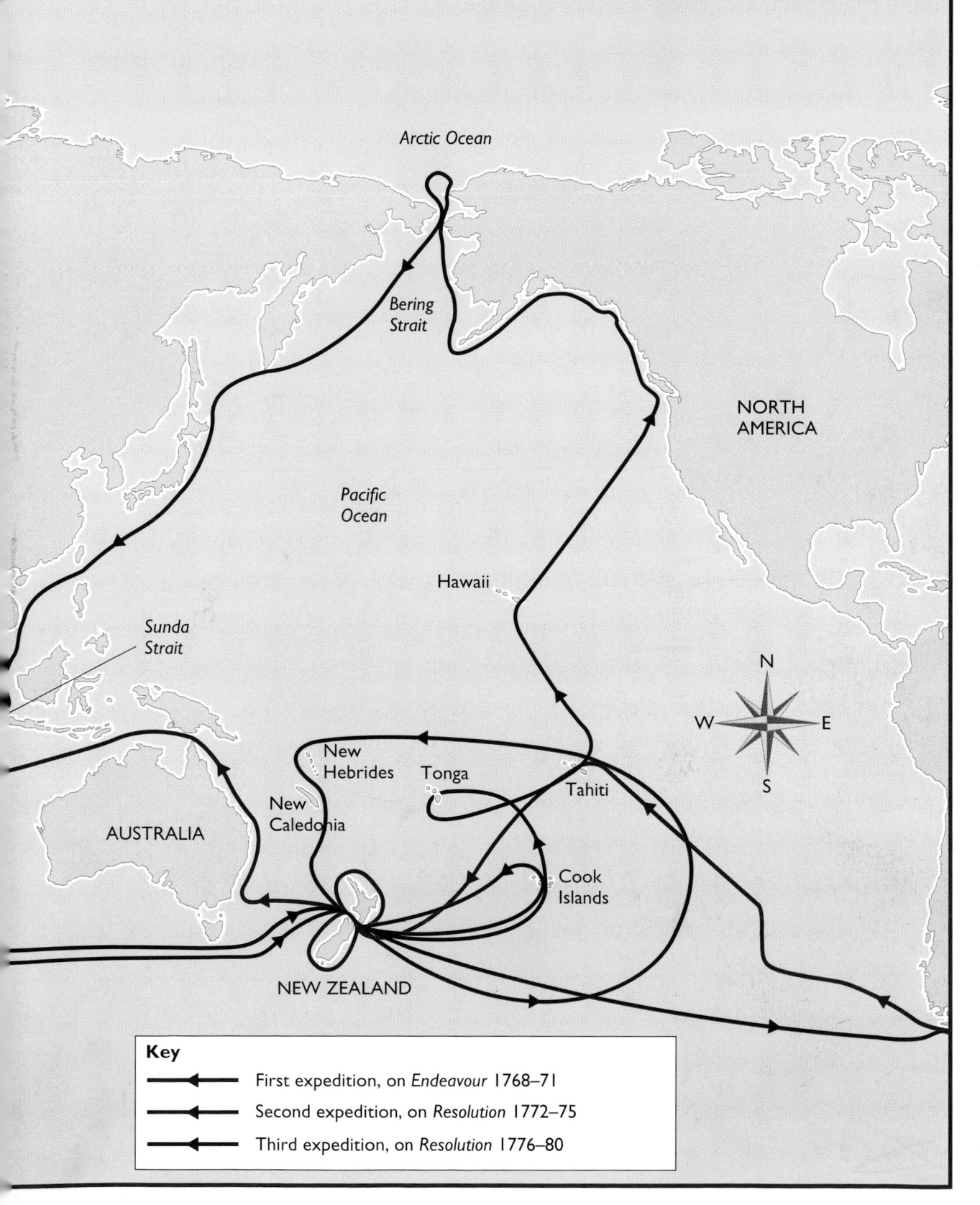

Arctic Ocean

Bering
Strait

NORTH
AMERICA

Pacific
Ocean

Hawaii

Sunda
Strait

N

W   E

S

New
Hebrides

Tonga

Tahiti

New
Caledonia

AUSTRALIA

Cook
Islands

NEW ZEALAND

Key

← First expedition, on *Endeavour* 1768–71

← Second expedition, on *Resolution* 1772–75

← Third expedition, on *Resolution* 1776–80

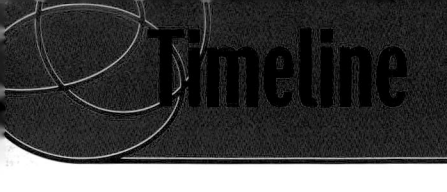

1728	James Cook born at Marton in Yorkshire.
1735	Family move to Great Ayton.
1741	Cook leaves school, **apprenticed** to Sanderson's general stores, in Staithes.
1746	Goes to sea. He is apprenticed to ship owners Walker Brothers of Whitby. He sails on **colliers** up and down the east coast of England.
1747	Is a servant aboard the *Freelove*.
1749	Promoted to seaman, he sails aboard various Walker colliers.
1752	Promoted to **mate** on the *Friendship*.
1755	Volunteers for the Royal Navy.
1757	Promoted to **master** of the *Pembroke*.
1759	Master of the *Northumberland*.
1760	Charts the St Lawrence River, Canada, often working at night close to enemy lines.
1762	Marries Elizabeth Batts while on leave in England.
1763	Surveys coast of Newfoundland and makes excellent **charts**. His reputation as a skilled **cartographer** is growing.
1767	Chosen to command voyage to South Seas to observe the transit of Venus, then carry out 'secret orders' to search for the 'great southern continent'.
1768	Sets sail on first voyage to South Seas in the *Endeavour*.
1769	Observes transit of Venus from Tahiti.
1770	Lands in eastern Australia and claims it for Britain.
1771	Returns to England.
1772	Sets sail with the *Resolution* and the *Adventure* on second voyage, to explore Antarctica.
1773	*Resolution* reaches its most southerly point in the Antarctic.
1775	Cook returns to England.
1776	Volunteers for third voyage. Sets sail with the *Resolution* and the *Discovery* to search for the North-west Passage that might link the Atlantic and Pacific oceans 'across the top' of northern Canada.
1778	Fails to find North-west Passage.
1779	James Cook killed at Hawaii.

Places to visit and further reading

Places to visit

The National Maritime Museum, Greenwich, London (has displays of many artefacts from Cook's expeditions, pictures painted on the voyages and a model of the *Endeavour*. You can visit the museum at www.nmm.ac.uk)

The Hunterian Museum, Glasgow, Scotland (has a collection of objects connected to Cook's voyages. You can visit the museum at www.hunterian.gla.ac.uk)

Armagh Observatory, College Hill, Armagh, N. Ireland (you can see original pages from Cook's **log** of his first voyage)

Website

CaptainCookStudyUnit.com (a huge site covering every aspect of Cook's life and voyages).

Further reading

Hatt, Christine: *The Settlement of Australia* (History in Writing series, Evans Books, 1999)

Rees, Rosemary, Styles, Sue and Hook, Adam: *Ships and Seafarers* (Heinemann Library, 1993)

Sources

Beaglehole, J.C: *The Journals of Captain Cook* (Cambridge University Press, various dates of publication, six volumes)

Grenfell Price, A.: *The Explorations of Captain Cook in the Pacific* (Angus and Robertson, London/Heritage Press, New York, 1969) (consists of extracts from Cook's log and journals)

Warner, Oliver: *Captain Cook and the South Pacific* (Cassell Caravell, London/ American Heritage Publishing, New York, 1963)

Aborigines inhabitants of Australia, whose descendants migrated there around 40,000 years before Cook's arrival

active service ships engaged in war and likely to attack or be attacked are on active service

Admiralty the commanders of the Royal Navy, based in London

alliances agreements between countries, often linked to fighting together in wars

apprentice young person bound by an agreement to a craftsman who will teach them a craft or trade

aristocracy those people born into rich or well-known families, who make up the highest class in society

astronomy study of the stars, carried out by astronomers

benefactor one who helps another person in some significant way

bow the front of the ship

capital offence crime or breach of military discipline punishable by death

cartographer maker of maps

charts maps, usually of sea

collier merchant ship specially built to transport coal

colonize establish a group of settlers in a new country

commission instruction promoting someone (usually naval or military) to the rank of officer

dysentery disease of the intestine, often fatal in Cook's time

engagement (in naval terms) a battle

flog punish by whipping, usually on the back. It was a standard form of discipline in the Navy in Cook's time. The whole crew were assembled to watch a flogging.

guineas unit of British money (sterling) equal to one pound and five pence. In Cook's time, it was the usual unit of measure in transactions between important people or 'gentlemen'.

icebergs floating islands of freshwater ice that have broken away from the frozen coast

latitude position of a place or ship in terms of how far north or south of the Equator it is. The horizontal (east–west) lines of latitude on a chart allow a captain to plot his position.

lieutenant naval officer ranked between seaman and captain

log the daily record of a ship, usually kept by the captain. It records the ship's position, the weather, technical notes and so on, but can also include such things as incidents with the crew, and sights seen. Cook's logs are particularly full of interesting details.

longboat small boat, like a modern-day lifeboat, carried by a larger ship, usually used to ferry crew to shore, to explore inlets and so on

longitude position of a place or ship in terms of how far east or west of the 'prime meridian' line (at Greenwich, London) it is. The vertical (north–south) lines of longitude on a chart allow a captain to plot his position.

Maori inhabitants of New Zealand

marine soldier who sailed as part of a ship's crew to fight the enemy in battle and maintain discipline among the sailors

master the captain of a merchant (non-naval) vessel. In the Navy, the master is the officer responsible for navigation.

mate ship's officer who sees that the captain's commands are carried out

merchant ship any non-naval vessel, freighter or trading ship

midshipman low-ranking naval officer

mutiny (mutinied) rebellion by a ship's crew (or any group of fighting men who disobey orders)

naturalist term used in Cook's day to describe someone who studies nature and natural phenomena. Modern science is usually more specific, dividing naturalists into botanists, biologists and so on.

non-commissioned describes an officer not holding any special commission

pack ice the sea freezing into a sheet of ice

pinnace small boat, usually rowed but also carrying a mast and sail

prize money every member of a Navy ship received a share of the money they obtained if they captured an enemy vessel then ransomed her or some of her crew, or sold her and her cargo

reef off-shore rocks, usually at least partly submerged and dangerous to ships

rigging spars and ropes controlling the sails on a sailing ship

Royal Society the most prestigious scientific society in Britain in Cook's day

scurvy painful, and in Cook's time often fatal disease, common among sailors on long voyages, caused by a lack of vitamin C

spars the wooden crosspieces on a mast from which sails are hung

stern the rear of a ship

transported in Britain in the 18th and 19th centuries, convicted criminals could be transported, or sent, by ship to prison colonies in Australia to serve their sentences. Conditions were appalling and many died either on the voyage or in Australia.

unseaworthy describes a ship too old or badly maintained to be sailed safely

Titles in the *Groundbreakers* series include:

Hardback   0 431 10489 1

Hardback   0 431 10490 5

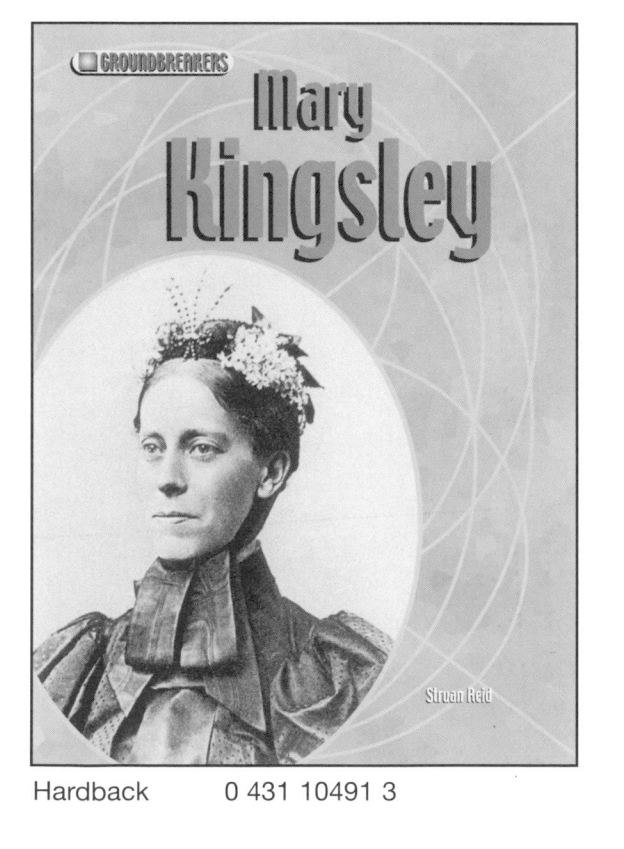

Hardback   0 431 10491 3

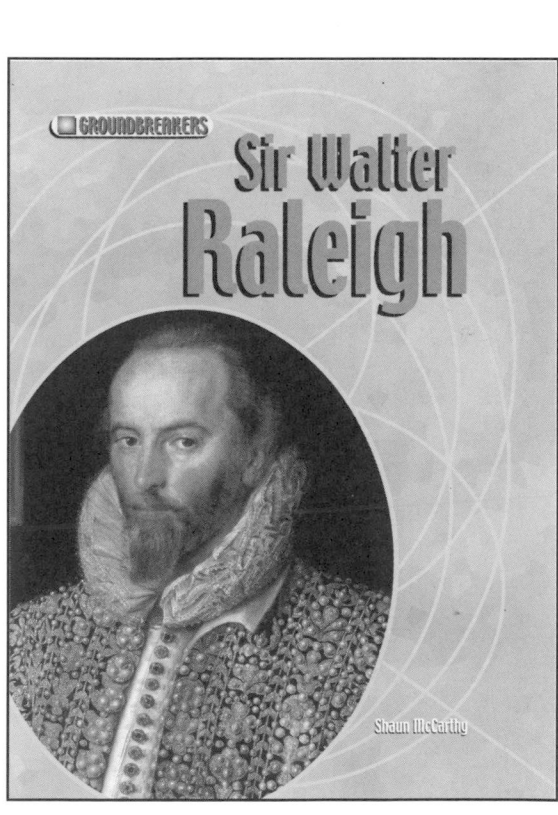

Hardback   0 431 10488 3

Find out about the other titles in this series on our website www.heinemann.co.uk/library